ASTRONAUT TRAVEL GUIDES

EARTH

NICK HUNTER

Heinemann
LIBRARY
Chicago, Illinois

www.capstonepub.com
Visit our website to find out more information about Heinemann-Raintree books.

To order:

☎ Phone 800-747-4992

▭ Visit www.capstonepub.com to browse our catalog and order online.

Edited by Nancy Dickmann and Laura Knowles
Designed by Steve Mead
Original illustrations © Capstone Global
   Library Ltd 2013
Picture research by Mica Brancic

Originated by Capstone Global Library Ltd
Printed and bound in the United States of America in North Mankato, Minnesota.
062014   008261RP

16 15 14
10 9 8 7 6 5 4

Library of Congress Cataloging-in-
**   Publication Data**
Hunter, Nick.
Earth / Nick Hunter.—1st ed.
 p. cm.—(Astronaut travel guides)
Includes bibliographical references and index.
ISBN 978-1-4109-4568-6 (hb)—ISBN 978-1-4109-4577-8 (pb) 1. Earth—Juvenile literature. I. Title.
QB631.4.H86 2013

   550—dc23   2011038926

Acknowledgements
We would like to thank the following for permission to reproduce photographs: Alamy p. 32 (© Bruce Coleman Inc./Kay & Karl Ammann); Corbis pp. 19 (EPA/Asahi Shimbun/© STR), 29 (© Kennan Ward), 31 (ZUMA Press/The Commercial Appeal/© Mike Maple), 33 (Aurora Photos/© Axel M. Cipollini), 37 (© Frans Lanting); ESA p. 5 bottom, 34; Getty Images p. 26 (Time & Life Pictures/Alfred Eisenstaedt); iStockphoto p. 12 (© Marcio Silva); Mark Thompson p. 14; NASA p. 4 (Johnson Space Center), 7 (Jet Propulsion Laboratory), 8 (ESA, and M. Livio and the Hubble 20th Anniversary Team (STScI)); NASA pp. 10, 17 (JPL/UCSD/JSC), 30 (Goddard Space Flight Center/Scientific Visualization Studio, and Hal Pierce (SSAI), who developed the original treatment.), 5 top and 9 (Bill Ingalls); Science Photo Library, pp. 22 (John Beatty), 38 (NASA/GSFC/Scientific Visualization Studio); Shutterstock pp. 11 (© Olinchuk), 20 (© Axel2001) 21 (© Somchaij), 24 (© Reistlin Magere) 25 (© Photography Perspectives - Jeff Smith), 40-41 (© Martiin || Fluidworkshop), 5 middle and 27 (© Goran cakmazovic).

Design image elements reproduced with permission of Shutterstock/© Hunor Focze/© Marcel Clemens/© Sergei Butorin/© Van Hart/© Zhanna Ocheret

Cover photograph of a night view of North America from the satellite to the glowing lights of towns on the sunrise from the east reproduced with permission of Shutterstock/© Anton Balazh.

We would like to thank Mark Thompson, Paolo Nespoli, and ESA for their invaluable help in the preparation of this book.

CONTENTS

Some words are shown in bold, **like this**. You can find out what they mean by looking in the glossary.

DON'T FORGET

These boxes will remind you what you need to take with you on your big adventure.

NUMBER CRUNCHING

Don't miss these little chunks of data as you speed through the travel guide!

AMAZING FACTS

You need to know these fascinating facts to get the most out of your space safari!

WHO'S WHO?

Find out about the space explorers who have studied the universe in the past and today.

PREPARE FOR LANDING!

Imagine you are visiting Earth from outer space. After traveling through the vastness of space, Earth will be a good place to land. No matter which faraway **planet** you are arriving from, the blue oceans of Earth look very inviting after a long journey.

As you approach Earth, you will see the blue oceans and the brown and green land covering the planet's surface.

OTHER DESTINATIONS?

On the way to Earth, you may have passed some of the other planets in our **solar system**. There are eight planets that **orbit** the Sun. Giant **gas** planets, such as Jupiter and Saturn, are great to look at, but you could not land on them—they do not even have solid surfaces! Mercury and Venus are closer to the Sun and far too hot. The red planet Mars does not have water on the surface like Earth. Mars also has almost no **atmosphere**, which makes it very cold.

Earth is surrounded by an atmosphere made up of gases, such as **oxygen** and nitrogen. This atmosphere is very important in making Earth such a great place to visit, but it can be a problem when landing a spacecraft. Make sure your spacecraft can stand the intense heat you will experience when you hurtle into the atmosphere from space.

See page 9 to find out why spacecraft need powerful rockets.

Find out about Earth's life-forms on page 26.

Meet astronaut Paolo Nespoli on page 34.

DON'T FORGET

Here are a couple of things you should pack for your journey to Earth:

- a life raft, in case you land in water
- solar panels, so you can capture the Sun's **energy** to power your spacecraft and other equipment.

THIRD PLANET FROM THE SUN

If you are traveling from a planet circling another star, it will take you many years to reach Earth, even if you can travel close to the speed of light. The closest star to Earth, apart from the Sun, is four **light years** away. This means that light from it takes four years to reach Earth. If you head toward the Sun, Earth is the third planet away from it.

NUMBER CRUNCHING

Earth is the biggest of the four rocky planets close to the Sun, measuring 7,926 miles (12,756 kilometers) across at the **equator**. Jupiter is the largest planet in the solar system; Earth could fit inside it about 1,000 times.

SET YOUR CLOCK

Earth is not always in the same place. It travels around the Sun. This orbit takes just over 365 days. These 365 days are called a year and, because the orbit takes a little more than 365 days, an extra day is added to the calendar every four years to make a leap year.

Earth also spins around on its own **axis** every 24 hours. During that time, every part of Earth spends some time facing the Sun and some time facing away, so it is in darkness. The light time is called day and the dark time is night.

Earth travels at 67,000 miles (108,000 kilometers) per hour on its journey around the Sun.

The Moon orbits Earth. It is a good place for a day trip while you are visiting.

Earth, like all planets, was formed from a cloud of dust and gases called a nebula. Over millions of years, the tiny fragments of **matter** in a nebula came together to form the Sun. A swirling disc of matter around the Sun eventually formed Earth and the other planets.

Nebulas like this one will form stars and planets over billions of years. This nebula is more than 6,000 light years from Earth.

PULLING IT ALL TOGETHER

The planets were formed by a force called **gravity**. Gravity is present everywhere in the universe. Every object pulls other objects toward it because of gravity. We do not really notice this force, except with objects that have a really huge **mass**, such as planets and stars. Gravity is also the force that will pull your spacecraft toward Earth. It attracts everything near the planet toward it, including the gases of Earth's atmosphere.

As the solar system formed, the parts of the swirling disc of matter closest to the Sun contained more rock, while the more distant parts of the disc were mainly ice. Because of this, Earth and the other planets closer to the Sun were made mainly of rock.

NUMBER CRUNCHING

In the 1600s, scholars believed that Earth was about 6,000 years old. By the late 1800s, advances in science meant that scientists thought Earth was at least hundreds of millions of years old. **Astronomers** now think that Earth and the rest of the solar system are 4.5 billion years old.

Spacecraft need powerful rockets to escape from Earth's gravity. Before coming to Earth, make sure that your spacecraft will be able to leave again.

THE YOUNG PLANET

You would not have wanted to travel to Earth when it was first formed. Bubbling hot seas of water began to form as the new planet's rocks cooled. The planet was probably bombarded by **comets** and **asteroids**, forming huge **craters** like the ones we can still see on the Moon.

Today, you will not be able to see much sign of the craters caused by these huge rocks, as other forces have shaped Earth's surface over billions of years. However, comets may have had a positive effect on Earth. Comets contain water in the form of ice, and they may have brought much of the water that fills Earth's oceans.

Because so much of Earth's surface is covered by oceans, there is a good chance that you will land in water. This spacecraft is using parachutes to land in the sea.

DRIFTING CONTINENTS

Unlike other planets, Earth's surface is made up of lots of interlocking plates, like a cracked eggshell. If you want to visit Earth's oldest rocks, you probably need to head for northern Canada or Greenland. Earth's land has changed a lot over billions of years. About 250 million years ago, the land on Earth was all part of one big land mass. Over millions of years, parts of this land mass drifted apart to form Earth's different **continents**. They are still moving now, but only about 2 to 4 inches (5 to 10 centimeters) every year.

From space, you will be able to see how the continents of South America and Africa once fit together.

If you shortened the history of Earth into a single day, the first human-like creatures did not appear until almost one minute before midnight. All human civilization took place in the last one-tenth of a second.

LIFE ON EARTH

Almost 1 billion years after Earth first formed, something began to develop that has not been found on any other planet in the solar system—life. For around 3 billion years, simple **microorganisms** were the only life on Earth. The first animals started to develop about 500 million years ago. By about 200 million years ago, huge dinosaurs roamed the planet.

Fossils found in Earth's ancient rocks can tell us about the history of life on Earth.

MODERN LIFE

During Earth's long history, there have been several times when a large number of **species** of living things have disappeared in a very short time. These major changes could have been caused by the climate getting hotter or colder. They could also have been caused by huge volcanic eruptions or by asteroids that collided with the planet. The last of these changes took place about 65 million years ago. Modern animals and plants have developed since then. The first human-like creatures on two legs probably appeared by about 4 million years ago.

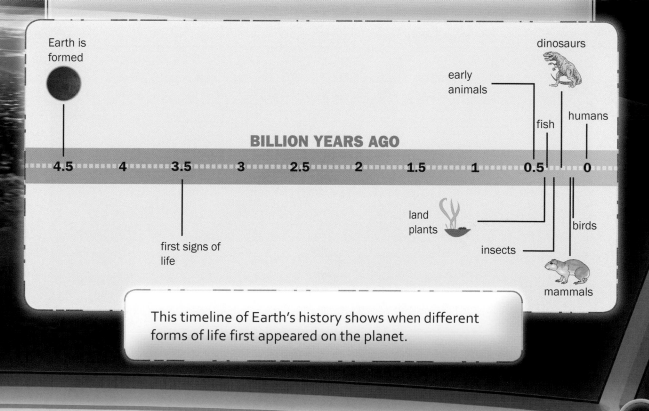

This timeline of Earth's history shows when different forms of life first appeared on the planet.

INTERVIEW WITH AN ASTRONOMER

Mark Thompson has been an amateur astronomer for 20 years. He has also hosted television shows about stars and space, helping adults and young people to understand the night sky.

Q *What's the most exciting thing that you've been able to see so far in space?*

A One thing was quite recently, and it was actually when the International Space Station went over. I pointed a telescope at the space station ... and I actually managed to see the solar panels and the structure of the thing. To see that through a telescope, when there were people on there—I mean, it was hard work following it because it was shifting pretty fast—but seeing a space station up in orbit, when I'd read about it and I'd seen it as a little speck of light, to actually see it as a space station was phenomenal. I think that it kind of brought space travel down to earth a little bit; made it all feel totally real.

Q *Do you think we will ever have human colonies in space?*

A Absolutely! Yes, yes, yes. Definitely, no doubt about it at all. We've been to the Moon, we've got the access to the orbit around the Earth [figured out] … I think it's a natural human desire to want to get out into the depths of the solar system and even further, I guess, and I think the only way we can do that is by colonizing space. As far as outside the solar system and beyond, then it will take a fair few thousand years, absolutely. But I think, in our own solar system, I think a Moon colony isn't that far off the mark, and I think some sort of Moon base will probably be the next big development in the world of space exploration … and that's going to happen in the next couple of hundred years, I'm pretty sure.

Q *Which historical astronomer would you most like to meet?*

A Probably it would have to be someone from quite a long, long while ago. There was a Greek Philosopher called Eratosthenes. He actually measured the circumference of Earth, and he did that by looking at the way sunlight hits Earth. I think what inspires me most is the **ingenuity** of people who had no computers, had no technology to help them; they've worked stuff out by thinking about stuff.

Q *Why do you think it's important to study space?*

A I think it helps to ground humans, and by that I mean it kind of keeps you focused on where we are in the world … But also, there's a lot of stuff that's come from space exploration that has helped people down on Earth. A good example of that is the water purification system that is used on the space station. The technology that was used for that is now being used in the developing world to help purify water for people that are in nations that don't have a lot of water. So, there are a lot of technological advances that come out of space exploration, which have helped people here on Earth.

SEEING THE SIGHTS

There is plenty to see on your visit to Earth. One of the most important things is often forgotten by people who live on Earth, because it is all around them.

AMAZING FACTS

The atmosphere shields Earth from asteroids. Asteroids can travel as fast as 28 miles (45 kilometers) per second. When the smaller of these lumps of space rock hit the atmosphere, they become very hot, and most are broken up before they can hit the ground.

GREAT ATMOSPHERE

Earth's atmosphere is one of the first things you will notice as you approach the planet. From space, it looks like a thin, blue shell around the planet. Earth is lucky to have its atmosphere. Mercury and Mars have almost no atmosphere, and Venus's atmosphere is poisonous. Earth's atmosphere is a mix of several gases, mainly nitrogen and oxygen. Oxygen is essential for animals and plants to breathe.

The mix of gases in the atmosphere also helps to keep Earth at the right temperature for living things. The atmosphere stops too much of the Sun's energy from reaching Earth's surface. It also acts like a blanket, to prevent the Sun's energy from escaping back into space.

The atmosphere helps to protect Earth from the Sun's harmful **radiation**.

NUMBER CRUNCHING

Earth's atmosphere extends about 370 miles (600 kilometers) into space, but the upper levels are very thin and cold. The troposphere is the part of the atmosphere that extends from the surface of Earth for about 12 miles (19 kilometers). This is the only part of the atmosphere that contains enough oxygen to support living things.

ON THE SURFACE

When your spacecraft lands, you will be on Earth's **crust**. This feels fairly solid, but it may not be quite as fixed as you think. Earth's crust is actually made up of a series of huge, rocky plates that cover the whole planet. The crust is 45 miles (75 kilometers) thick in places, but it can be as little as 3 miles (5 kilometers) thick beneath the bottom of the oceans. The plates are made of many different types of rock. These rocks have been formed by a combination of heat and **pressure** beneath the crust.

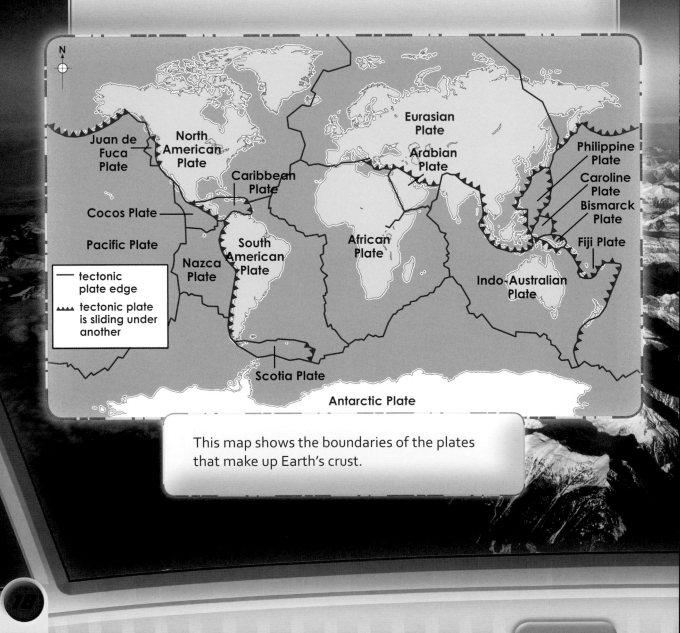

N

Eurasian Plate

Juan de Fuca Plate

North American Plate

Arabian Plate

Philippine Plate

Caribbean Plate

Caroline Plate

Cocos Plate

Bismarck Plate

Pacific Plate

South American Plate

African Plate

Fiji Plate

Nazca Plate

Indo-Australian Plate

—— tectonic plate edge

▲▲▲ tectonic plate is sliding under another

Scotia Plate

Antarctic Plate

This map shows the boundaries of the plates that make up Earth's crust.

Over millions of years, the movements of these plates have shaped much of Earth's surface. Where plates collide, the ground gets pushed upward, creating mountain ranges.

EARTHQUAKES

Most of these movements happen very slowly, with plates moving by a few inches every year. However, plates can also move suddenly. When this happens, it causes an earthquake, which is one of the most destructive events that can happen on Earth. Earthquakes on land cause buildings and bridges to collapse. When an earthquake strikes beneath the ocean, it can produce an enormous wave called a tsunami.

WHO'S WHO?

In 1912, Alfred Wegener (1880–1930) was the first person to suggest that the continents had once been part of a super-continent called Pangaea. This led to the idea that Earth's crust was made up of a series of interlocking plates, a bit like a jigsaw puzzle.

In 2011, the coast of northern Japan was hit by a huge tsunami. The tsunami was so strong that it pushed boats onto the land.

The Himalayas are the tallest mountains in the world. They were formed by the collision of two of Earth's plates about 40 to 50 million years ago. The mountains are still growing by about 0.5 inch (1 centimeter) every year.

EXPLORING THE LAND

The crust has been shaped by more than moving plates. The changing weather has often worked together with water to give Earth a landscape like no other planet.

Depending on where you land, you could find yourself in many different landscapes. Landing in Antarctica or the Arctic would give you a chance to see the icecaps—large sheets of ice that are over a mile thick in places. Much more of the planet used to be covered by ice, and this has helped to shape the landscape.

Mount Everest in the Himalayas is Earth's highest mountain. You will need to take oxygen with you, since the air is very thin at around 5.5 miles (8.8 kilometers) above sea level.

Elsewhere on Earth, the impact of weather and water can clearly be seen. Ocean waves carve out cliffs and bays. Away from the coast, rivers wind their way through the landscape. Even in dry deserts, rivers can create steep-sided valleys called canyons.

Any visitor to Earth should see the Grand Canyon in Arizona. It was carved out by the Colorado River, which flows at the bottom of this amazing canyon.

HUMAN IMPACT

If you arrive at night, you will see the lights of cities and roads crossing Earth's continents. You will also notice that large parts of Earth's land are used for growing crops and raising animals. Humans also dig rocks and **fossil fuels** out of the ground. If you know where to look, you can find oil, gold, and even diamonds.

BENEATH THE CRUST

One of the sights you can see on Earth's surface will give a clue to what lies beneath the crust. At the points where plates meet, volcanoes pour out **molten** rock, called lava, onto the surface. Sometimes these volcanoes will explode with amazing force.

The ash and lava come from beneath Earth's crust. The plates of the crust sit on the upper mantle, an area where the rock is just starting to become molten. The lower mantle is where the lava that pours out of volcanoes comes from. Under the ground, this molten rock is called magma. In addition to erupting from volcanoes, magma often seeps out onto the sea floor to form new rocks.

Iceland is known for its volcanic activity. It lies on the boundary between two plates.

Earth's core can be divided into two parts. The outer core is made of liquid iron and nickel. At the very center of the planet is a solid ball of iron or nickel. Although the temperature at the core is hot enough to melt metal, the metal core stays solid. This is because it is under so much pressure.

MAGNETIC EARTH

You cannot see Earth's core, but its influence is felt on the surface and beyond. This lump of metal makes Earth into a huge magnet. This magnet protects Earth from the Sun's harmful radiation.

Earth's crust is only a thin layer covering the molten rocks beneath it. Temperatures in the core are hotter than the surface of the Sun.

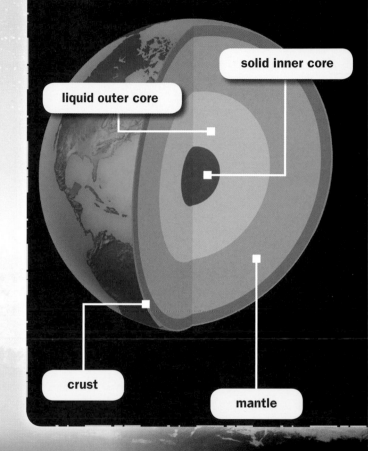

solid inner core

liquid outer core

crust

mantle

DON'T FORGET

Bring a **magnetic** compass with you! Earth's magnetic core means a compass will always point in a north–south direction. A compass will help you find your way around the world if you get lost.

SUPPORTING LIFE

Scientists have not been able to find any other planets or moons in the solar system that have all the ingredients necessary to support life. What is it that makes Earth such a unique place for life to develop?

Earth is neither too close nor too far from the Sun. Being close to the Sun makes Mercury and Venus unbearably hot. Planets farther away from the Sun are much too cold to support life similar to that found on Earth.

This rich rain forest **habitat** depends on the heat of the Sun and water falling as rain to support a huge variety of life.

Even Earth's deserts have a tiny amount of water. Without water, living things cannot survive.

PRESENCE OF WATER

Earth's climate brings one huge benefit above all others. It allows water to exist in liquid form. All life as we know it needs water. Other planets, such as Mars, may once have had liquid water, and they still have ice on parts of their surfaces.

Water remains on Earth because the planet's atmosphere prevents it from being lost to space. The atmosphere and Earth's magnetic field protect the planet, so life has been able to develop.

DON'T FORGET

If you want to find living things on a planet, you need to look for:

- The gases carbon, nitrogen, oxygen, and hydrogen: Living things are made of many different ingredients, and these are the most important.
- Energy: Most energy on Earth comes from the Sun. This energy helps plants to grow and to provide food for other living things.
- Water: As far as we know, all life needs liquid water to develop.

LIFE ON EARTH

Life on Earth ranges from tiny single-**celled** organisms to enormous creatures such as the blue whale. Some organisms live for only a short time, but some trees live for thousands of years.

This huge variety of life on Earth has developed over billions of years. The living things that have adapted best to their environment pass on their features to the next generation. Living things that do not have those features do not survive. Over many generations, this leads to animals taking on many new features. It also leads to the appearance of new species of animals and plants.

WHO'S WHO?

Rachel Carson (1907–1964) led the way in the movement to protect Earth's environment. In her book *Silent Spring* (1962), Carson pointed out the damage that chemicals used in agriculture could cause in the wider environment.

DEPENDING ON EACH OTHER

The different forms of life on Earth also depend on each other and on the environments in which they live. Humans and animals feed on plants and other animals to get the energy they need to live. Green plants even help to put more oxygen into Earth's atmosphere by the way they make food. Living things then breathe in this oxygen.

Bees depend on flowers for their food. In return, they help plants to reproduce, by spreading pollen from one plant to another.

AMAZING FACTS

A report in 2010 estimated that animal populations had fallen by 30 percent since 1970. Much of this was due to human activities, such as turning habitats into farmland.

WHEN TO GO

One of the things that makes Earth such a great place to visit is the climate. For the most part, Earth's climate is quite pleasant, especially when compared to the extreme heat and cold of other planets.

CHANGING SEASONS

Earth's weather systems are powered by the Sun's energy, as the planet makes its year-long journey around the star. Earth is tilted on its axis, so that different parts of the planet are facing toward the Sun at different times of the year. When it is summer in the northern **hemisphere**, it is winter in the southern hemisphere. The changing seasons are necessary to grow plants and produce food for people and animals.

spring: northern hemisphere
fall: southern hemisphere

winter: northern hemisphere
summer: southern hemisphere

summer: northern hemisphere
winter: southern hemisphere

fall: northern hemisphere
spring: southern hemisphere

This diagram shows how some places receive more sunlight at different times of the year.

CLIMATE CHANGE

The delicate balance of gases in its atmosphere gives Earth its climate. Over billions of years, this balance has changed many times, and the climate has become much warmer or colder. In modern times, gases released into the atmosphere by human industry and vehicles mean that the atmosphere is trapping more of the Sun's energy. This is causing Earth's climate to grow warmer. Scientists believe that climate change could lead to serious problems for life on Earth.

NUMBER CRUNCHING

Earth's weather can be extreme. The highest temperature ever recorded was 134 degrees Fahrenheit (57 degrees Celsius), in the Libyan Desert. The lowest temperature ever recorded on Earth was −128 degrees Fahrenheit (−89 degrees Celsius), in Antarctica.

Earth's tilt on its axis means that, in summer, the Sun never sets close to the North Pole. This photo shows the changing position of the Sun through the night.

WATCH THE WEATHER

Most places on Earth do not have the same weather all the time. Weather systems are driven by energy from the Sun and vary depending on Earth's tilt in its journey around the Sun. Weather patterns are also affected by Earth's own rotation and the oceans.

DON'T FORGET

Depending on where you land and the time of year, the weather can be very unpredictable. Make sure you bring clothes for everything from extreme heat to bitterly cold weather.

The oceans help to make the world's weather less extreme, as they stay cool in summer and warmer than frozen land in the winter. They are also at the center of the water cycle, which provides water for all living things on Earth.

hurricane

Hurricanes can be seen from space.

EXTREME WEATHER

Earth is no stranger to extremes of weather, and because the planet is so crowded, this can be disastrous for humans and animals. You may be able to see some of these extremes before you land. Hurricanes and typhoons are violent spinning storms. Hurricanes are one possible cause of floods that can affect whole countries. Earth's storms are still less extreme than those found on some other planets. For example, Jupiter's Great Red Spot is actually a huge storm that has raged for hundreds of years.

AMAZING FACTS

Tornadoes are the most destructive storms on Earth. Although these spinning funnels of air only cause devastation over a very narrow path, winds can reach speeds of around 300 miles (480 kilometers) per hour.

A devastating tornado hit the town of Joplin, Missouri, in May 2011, killing 159 people.

PEOPLE WORTH MEETING

You will not have trouble finding people to come with you on your trip to Earth. It is the best place to visit—at least in this solar system. When you get here, you will want to track down some people to explain the planet to you.

CREW MEMBER:

NEIL ARMSTRONG (BORN 1930-2012)

Armstrong is one of only 12 people from Earth to have landed on another world—the Moon. He will be able to tell you about space travel from Earth's point of view.

EXPERT KNOWLEDGE:

Space travel and the Moon

CREW MEMBER:

JANE GOODALL (BORN 1934)

Any visitor to Earth needs to understand the variety of life on Earth. Jane Goodall spent much of her life studying chimpanzees in Africa, building a detailed knowledge of their behavior.

EXPERT KNOWLEDGE:

Animal and environment expert

CREW MEMBER:

ROBERT BALLARD (BORN 1942)

Humans have explored most of planet Earth. However, there are still parts of the deepest oceans that have not been fully explored. Ballard has probably explored more of the oceans than anyone else, using underwater vehicles to study wrecks and undersea life.

EXPERT KNOWLEDGE:

Ocean explorer

CREW MEMBER:

VOLCANOLOGIST

If you want to find out more about what goes on inside the planet, find a volcanologist, who studies volcanoes and lava.

EXPERT KNOWLEDGE:

Looking beneath Earth's crust

CREW MEMBER:

METEOROLOGIST

A meteorologist studies the weather and would be able to tell you the best places to go to avoid extreme weather. He or she could also explain how to predict the weather.

EXPERT KNOWLEDGE:

Weather forecasting

INTERVIEW WITH AN ASTRONAUT

Paolo Nespoli is an Italian astronaut with the **European Space Agency (ESA)**. He enjoys scuba diving, flying airplanes, and photography. In 2007, Paolo went into space for 15 days, and in 2010 he spent 6 more months in space. In total, he has orbited Earth an amazing 2,782 times.

Q *When you're up on the International Space Station, what sorts of things can you see?*

A On the station there are several windows that are positioned so that they give us a good view of the Earth … it takes about 90 minutes to completely go around the Earth, which makes it difficult to look at anything on the sky because it changes continuously. I was able to see some of the major constellations … but it's pretty difficult, because it changes and goes.

So what we mostly looked at was actually Earth, and there we really were able to see a lot of things … I was fortunate enough that I saw an *Ariane* rocket taking off, leaving the atmosphere and bringing one of our supply vehicles. I was lucky enough to see it coming up out of the atmosphere toward the sky. That was pretty impressive.

Q *What is it like to see Earth from space?*

A Looking at the Earth is very spectacular from up there. We have this cupola [observatory] that allows us a big view of the Earth, and we spend much time there ... It's amazing— because you are spinning around the Earth at that speed— it's amazing how you can start from the scorching desert of Africa, and then 10 or 15 minutes later you are in Siberia looking at the deep snow, and then another 10 minutes later you are in China or you are down in Australia or in the Caribbean, with the blue ocean. I have taken pictures ... if I had tried to do that on Earth it would have taken a year or more just to capture all these things.

Q *Even with months in space, do you ever get tired of that view?*

A No, no! I think every time you look, you look and you find something different. It's just interesting, it's just amazing! And sometimes it is irritating, because you cannot find certain things.

I remember one day they asked us to take some pictures of Mount Kilimanjaro because they wanted to check the snow coverage and vegetation coverage ... and we flew all over Africa, and we could never find Kilimanjaro. So we were dumbfounded and were like, "We did not find Kilimanjaro! We did not see it! How is this possible that we lost Kilimanjaro?" But we lost it; we could not find it. So, it's amazing sometimes.

LIVING ON EARTH

So, now that you know a little more about planet Earth, do you think you could live here? Earth certainly has its dangers, from earthquakes and volcanoes to extreme weather, but it is still a better place for life than any other planet in the solar system.

WHERE NOT TO LIVE

Not everywhere on Earth is an ideal place to live. The frozen continent of Antarctica is covered in a thick layer of ice and is extremely cold, particularly in the middle of the continent. Perhaps the worst place to live on Earth would be at the bottom of the ocean. Little of the Sun's energy reaches the dark depths of the ocean. The microorganisms that live down there get their energy from volcanic vents in the ocean floor.

AMAZING FACTS

People on Earth are trying to find out if there is life on other planets. The Kepler Telescope watches more than 100,000 stars to see if there are planets like Earth orbiting around them. The project has discovered hundreds of solar systems with planets orbiting a star as well as dozens of planets that may contain life.

This crater in Australia was caused by the impact of an asteroid.

DON'T FORGET

Although Earth seems very safe, there are some dangers that come from outside the planet:

- The Sun's energy: Even though Earth's atmosphere protects it from the worst radiation, some harmful radiation still reaches the surface. You should wear sunscreen to protect you from the Sun.

- Asteroids: Small asteroids often land on Earth, and larger ones could be catastrophic. Astronomers are always looking for asteroids that might hit Earth.

A CHANGING PLANET

Although Earth is perfectly suited for life now, this may change in the future. We know that planets can change. Astronomers believe that the planet Mars once had liquid water and an atmosphere, but these were lost millions of years ago. There have been many times in Earth's history when many species of living things have become **extinct** in quite a short time. A major change in climate or the effects of an asteroid hitting Earth may have caused the death of the dinosaurs about 65 million years ago.

ice

This picture shows the ice around the North Pole. The amount of ice is getting smaller because of climate change. Melting ice could cause sea levels to rise and Earth's climate to change even faster.

Earth's climate has changed many times in the past, as the balance of gases in the atmosphere has changed. Earth's climate is currently getting warmer, as human activity is changing the balance of gases in the atmosphere. Humans are also changing the planet in other ways. Scientists believe that there is a risk of many species in the oceans becoming extinct because of over-fishing, pollution, and climate change.

FINDING SOLUTIONS

Humans will need to find solutions to these problems if Earth is to continue to support its growing population. So, when you have seen what Earth has to offer and decide to leave the planet, please take your trash home with you!

NUMBER CRUNCHING

Earth is a crowded planet. There are currently just over 7 billion people living on Earth. The population has almost doubled since 1970, and Earth will be home to more than 9 billion people by 2050. This growing population will continue to put pressure on Earth's fragile environment.

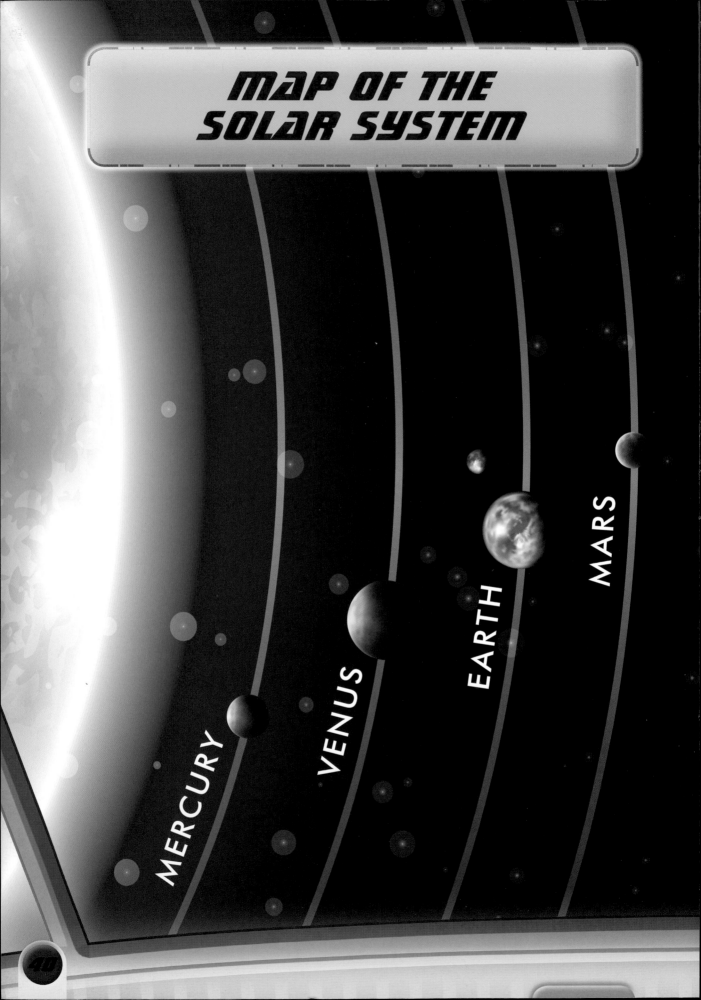

MAP OF THE SOLAR SYSTEM

MERCURY

VENUS

EARTH

MARS

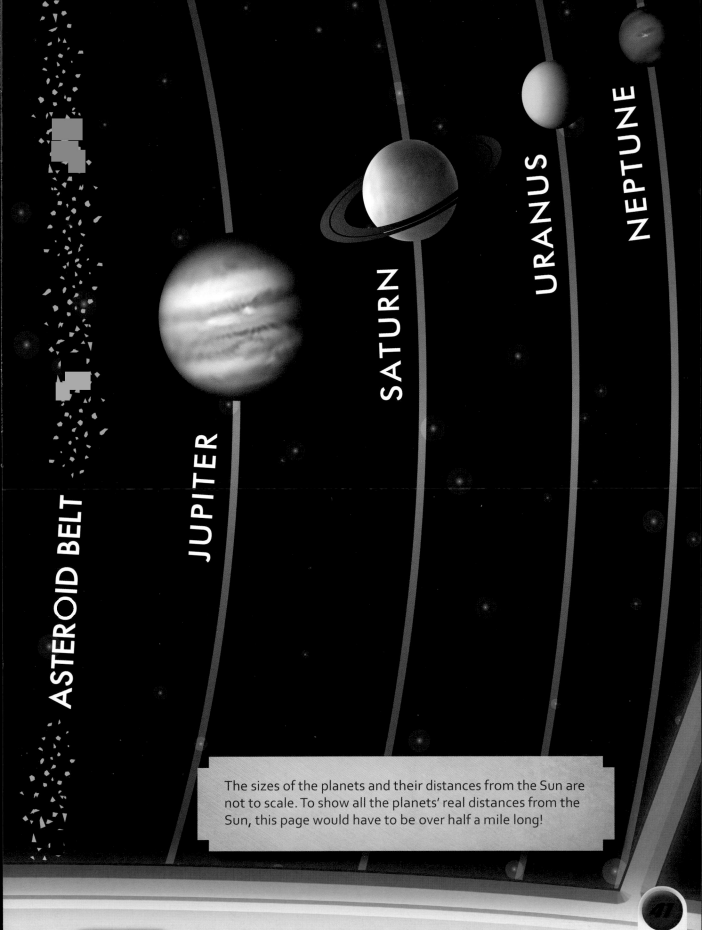

ASTEROID BELT

JUPITER

SATURN

URANUS

NEPTUNE

The sizes of the planets and their distances from the Sun are not to scale. To show all the planets' real distances from the Sun, this page would have to be over half a mile long!

TIMELINE

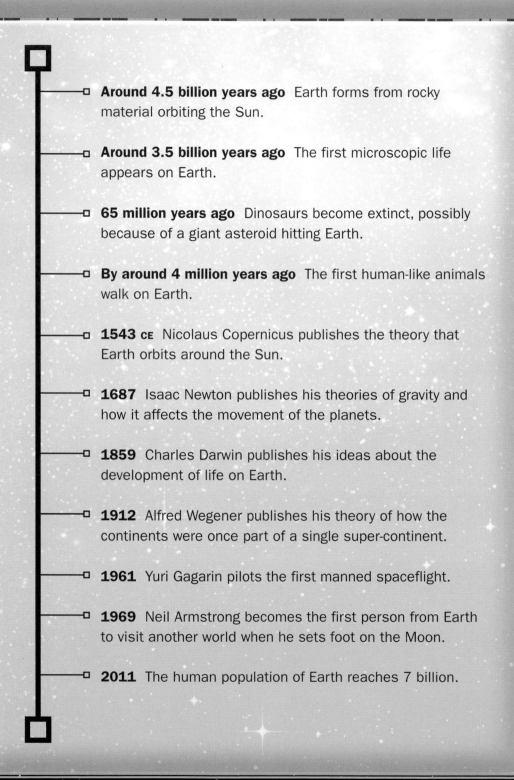

Around 4.5 billion years ago Earth forms from rocky material orbiting the Sun.

Around 3.5 billion years ago The first microscopic life appears on Earth.

65 million years ago Dinosaurs become extinct, possibly because of a giant asteroid hitting Earth.

By around 4 million years ago The first human-like animals walk on Earth.

1543 CE Nicolaus Copernicus publishes the theory that Earth orbits around the Sun.

1687 Isaac Newton publishes his theories of gravity and how it affects the movement of the planets.

1859 Charles Darwin publishes his ideas about the development of life on Earth.

1912 Alfred Wegener publishes his theory of how the continents were once part of a single super-continent.

1961 Yuri Gagarin pilots the first manned spaceflight.

1969 Neil Armstrong becomes the first person from Earth to visit another world when he sets foot on the Moon.

2011 The human population of Earth reaches 7 billion.

FACT FILE

POSITION:
93,000,000 miles (150,000,000 kilometers) from the Sun

ORBIT:
Orbits the Sun every 365.25 days (365 days = 1 year)

SIZE:
7,926 miles (12,756 kilometers) in diameter at the equator

MASS:
13,200,000,000,000,000,000,000,000 pounds

TEMPERATURE:
- Surface: Average 59 degrees Fahrenheit (15 degrees Celsius)
- Core: Up to 12,100 degrees Fahrenheit (6,700 degrees Celsius)

ATMOSPHERE:
Nitrogen: 78%; oxygen: 21%; other gases, including carbon dioxide: 1%

ROTATION:
Rotates on its axis every 23 hours, 56 minutes (24 hours = 1 day)

SATELLITES:
The Moon orbits Earth at a distance of 239,000 miles (384,000 kilometers)

GLOSSARY

adapt change to suit the surroundings or environment

asteroid lump of rock and metal that orbits the Sun and can be many miles across

astronomer scientist who studies space, stars, and planets

atmosphere layer of gases surrounding a planet

axis imaginary line around which something spins, such as a planet

cell small, usually microscopic, structure from which living things are made

comet object made of rock and ice that orbits the Sun

continent one of Earth's seven large areas of land

crater hole made by impact—for example, by an asteroid

crust solid, rocky outer layer of Earth

energy capacity to do work—for example, heat energy from the Sun warms Earth

equator imaginary line around the middle of a star or planet

European Space Agency (ESA) European organization involved in space research and exploration

extinct no longer living

fossil remains of a living thing preserved in rock, such as a dinosaur bone

fossil fuel fuels—oil, coal, and natural gas—formed over millions of years from the remains of living things

gas matter, such as oxygen, that is able to expand without limit unless it is contained

gravity force that acts between all objects to pull them together

habitat place or environment where an animal or plant usually lives

hemisphere half of Earth

ingenuity using your imagination and being inventive

light year unit used to make it easier to measure large distances. One light year is equal to 6 trillion miles—the distance that light travels in a year.

magnetic force that attracts or repels magnetic materials such as metal

mass amount of material that makes up an object

matter anything that has mass and fills space, including solids, liquids, and gases

microorganism living thing that can only be seen through a microscope

molten solid that has melted to become liquid

orbit path of an object around a star or planet

oxygen gas present in Earth's atmosphere that most living things need to breathe

planet large object that orbits a star

pressure pushing force on an object from something touching it, such as the pushing force of the air on our bodies

radiation tiny particles given out by the Sun

reproduce produce offspring

solar system the Sun, the planets, and other objects that are in orbit around the Sun

species type of animal or plant in which all members share most of the same characteristics

FIND OUT MORE

BOOKS

Biskup, Agnieszka. *Understanding Global Warming* (Graphic Expeditions). Mankato, Minn.: Capstone, 2008.

Bond, Peter. *DK Guide to Space* (DK Guides). New York: Dorling Kindersley, 2006.

Sparrow, Giles. *Earth and the Inner Planets* (Space Travel Guides). Mankato, Minn.: Smart Apple Media, 2012.

Spilsbury, Richard and Louise. *Minerals* (Let's Rock). Chicago: Heinemann Library, 2011.

Stott, Carole. *Space: From Earth to the Edge of the Universe*. New York: Dorling Kindersley, 2010.

INTERNET SITES

FactHound offers a safe, fun way to find internet sites related to this book. All of the sites on FactHound have been researched by our staff.

Here's all you do:

Visit *www.facthound.com*

Type in this code: 9781410945686

PLACES TO VISIT

Hayden Planetarium
Central Park West and 79th Street, New York, N.Y. 10024
www.haydenplanetarium.org

Smithsonian National Air and Space Museum
Independence Ave. at 7th St. SW, Washington, D.C. 20560
www.nasm.si.edu

SIGHTS TO SEE

Even if you live in a big city, you are probably not far from somewhere where you can see the forces that have shaped Earth. You may be close to some mountains where the plates of Earth's crust are colliding. Coastal landforms can also reveal the layers of Earth's rocks and how they have been shaped by weather and water. You may even be lucky enough to live near a place like the Grand Canyon.

FURTHER RESEARCH

- Earth, Sun, and Moon: Find out more about the relationship between Earth and the rest of the solar system. The Sun is essential for life on Earth, but the Moon also affects things like the tides of Earth's oceans.
- Volcanoes: These give us a window into the bubbling rock beneath Earth's crust. Find out about the different types of volcanoes and their enormous power.
- Climate change: Earth's climate is changing. What effects could this have, and what has happened when climate change has occurred in the past?